This Journal Belongs To

(A Badass B*tch Ready To Conquer Her Day!)

Go Slay Your Day!

A Badass B*tch has got to get her morning and night right as you are busy as f*ck and need to be ready to take on the World! You can't be doing that if you got sh*t on your mind bothering you. It will stop you from focusing and experiencing all the good sh*t you want to. Also, you won't be ready to face the challenging sh*t that always comes up!

This journal is designed to solve that!
In the morning there are 3 quick questions to clear your head of negativity, inspire positive thinking and prep for any challenges ahead of time.

In the night, there are three quick questions where you can note the good sh*t and bad sh*t of the day and prep for how tomorrow can be better.

Doing this everyday in the morning and night will help clear your head and give you a strong sense of direction for each day. It will also help you to quickly notice any patterns repeating over time so you can change sh*t up if you need to.
Consistency is key!

One Day at a Time...

Morning:

What do you need to express before you Kick the Sh*t out of this day?

What Good Sh*t do you want to feel during the day?

Challenges you expect to face? How can you handle them?

Night:

What was the Good Sh*t of the day?

What was the Bad Sh*t of the day?

How will i make tomorrow better?

She Believed She Could,
So She F*cking Did!

Morning:

What do you need to express before you Kick the Sh*t out of this day?

What Good Sh*t do you want to feel during the day?

Challenges you expect to face? How can you handle them?

Night:

What was the Good Sh*t of the day?

What was the Bad Sh*t of the day?

How will i make tomorrow better?

Morning:

What do you need to express before you Kick the Sh*t out of this day?

What Good Sh*t do you want to feel during the day?

Challenges you expect to face? How can you handle them?

Night:

What was the Good Sh*t of the day?

What was the Bad Sh*t of the day?

How will i make tomorrow better?

F*cking Go!

Morning:

What do you need to express before you Kick the Sh*t out of this day?

What Good Sh*t do you want to feel during the day?

Challenges you expect to face? How can you handle them?

Night:

What was the Good Sh*t of the day?

What was the Bad Sh*t of the day?

How will i make tomorrow better?

Morning:

What do you need to express before you Kick the Sh*t out of this day?

_____

What Good Sh*t do you want to feel during the day?

_____
_____

Challenges you expect to face? How can you handle them?

_____
_____

Night:

What was the Good Sh*t of the day?

_____
_____

What was the Bad Sh*t of the day?

_____
_____

How will i make tomorrow better?

_____
_____

To Try and Fail is ok. But Fail to try? You're Being a little B*tch.

Morning:

What do you need to express before you Kick the Sh*t out of this day?

What Good Sh*t do you want to feel during the day?

Challenges you expect to face? How can you handle them?

Night:

What was the Good Sh*t of the day?

What was the Bad Sh*t of the day?

How will i make tomorrow better?

Morning:

What do you need to express before you Kick the Sh*t out of this day?

What Good Sh*t do you want to feel during the day?

Challenges you expect to face? How can you handle them?

Night:

What was the Good Sh*t of the day?

What was the Bad Sh*t of the day?

How will i make tomorrow better?

What part of YOU will you share with the world today?

Morning:

What do you need to express before you Kick the Sh*t out of this day?

What Good Sh*t do you want to feel during the day?

Challenges you expect to face? How can you handle them?

Night:

What was the Good Sh*t of the day?

What was the Bad Sh*t of the day?

How will i make tomorrow better?

Morning:

What do you need to express before you Kick the Sh*t out of this day?

What Good Sh*t do you want to feel during the day?

Challenges you expect to face? How can you handle them?

Night:

What was the Good Sh*t of the day?

What was the Bad Sh*t of the day?

How will i make tomorrow better?

I Can and I Will, Watch Me!

Morning:

What do you need to express before you Kick the Sh*t out of this day?

What Good Sh*t do you want to feel during the day?

Challenges you expect to face? How can you handle them?

Night:

What was the Good Sh*t of the day?

What was the Bad Sh*t of the day?

How will i make tomorrow better?

Morning:

What do you need to express before you Kick the Sh*t out of this day?

What Good Sh*t do you want to feel during the day?

Challenges you expect to face? How can you handle them?

Night:

What was the Good Sh*t of the day?

What was the Bad Sh*t of the day?

How will i make tomorrow better?

You can do anything, but not everything.
Patience B*tch

Morning:

What do you need to express before you Kick the Sh*t out of this day?

What Good Sh*t do you want to feel during the day?

Challenges you expect to face? How can you handle them?

Night:

What was the Good Sh*t of the day?

What was the Bad Sh*t of the day?

How will i make tomorrow better?

Morning:

What do you need to express before you Kick the Sh*t out of this day?

What Good Sh*t do you want to feel during the day?

Challenges you expect to face? How can you handle them?

Night:

What was the Good Sh*t of the day?

What was the Bad Sh*t of the day?

How will i make tomorrow better?

You are Lovely.
Do You Believe It?

Morning:

What do you need to express before you Kick the Sh*t out of this day?

What Good Sh*t do you want to feel during the day?

Challenges you expect to face? How can you handle them?

Night:

What was the Good Sh*t of the day?

What was the Bad Sh*t of the day?

How will i make tomorrow better?

Morning:

What do you need to express before you Kick the Sh*t out of this day?

What Good Sh*t do you want to feel during the day?

Challenges you expect to face? How can you handle them?

Night:

What was the Good Sh*t of the day?

What was the Bad Sh*t of the day?

How will i make tomorrow better?

What if you Fall?
Yeah, but what if you F*cking Fly?!

Morning:

What do you need to express before you Kick the Sh*t out of this day?

What Good Sh*t do you want to feel during the day?

Challenges you expect to face? How can you handle them?

Night:

What was the Good Sh*t of the day?

What was the Bad Sh*t of the day?

How will i make tomorrow better?

Morning:

What do you need to express before you Kick the Sh*t out of this day?

What Good Sh*t do you want to feel during the day?

Challenges you expect to face? How can you handle them?

Night:

What was the Good Sh*t of the day?

What was the Bad Sh*t of the day?

How will i make tomorrow better?

You've Totally Got This!

Morning:

What do you need to express before you Kick the Sh*t out of this day?

_____

What Good Sh*t do you want to feel during the day?

_____

_____

Challenges you expect to face? How can you handle them?

_____

Night:

What was the Good Sh*t of the day?

_____

_____

What was the Bad Sh*t of the day?

_____

How will i make tomorrow better?

_____

_____

Morning:

What do you need to express before you Kick the Sh*t out of this day?

What Good Sh*t do you want to feel during the day?

Challenges you expect to face? How can you handle them?

Night:

What was the Good Sh*t of the day?

What was the Bad Sh*t of the day?

How will i make tomorrow better?

Life is Tough You Beautiful B*tch, But Damn, So Are You!

Morning:

What do you need to express before you Kick the Sh*t out of this day?

What Good Sh*t do you want to feel during the day?

Challenges you expect to face? How can you handle them?

Night:

What was the Good Sh*t of the day?

What was the Bad Sh*t of the day?

How will i make tomorrow better?

Morning:

What do you need to express before you Kick the Sh*t out of this day?

What Good Sh*t do you want to feel during the day?

Challenges you expect to face? How can you handle them?

Night:

What was the Good Sh*t of the day?

What was the Bad Sh*t of the day?

How will i make tomorrow better?

A Wise Woman Once Said "F*ck This Sh*t" and She Lived Happily Ever After!

Morning:

What do you need to express before you Kick the Sh*t out of this day?

What Good Sh*t do you want to feel during the day?

Challenges you expect to face? How can you handle them?

Night:

What was the Good Sh*t of the day?

What was the Bad Sh*t of the day?

How will i make tomorrow better?

Morning:

What do you need to express before you Kick the Sh*t out of this day?

What Good Sh*t do you want to feel during the day?

Challenges you expect to face? How can you handle them?

Night:

What was the Good Sh*t of the day?

What was the Bad Sh*t of the day?

How will i make tomorrow better?

She Needed a Hero...
So That's What She Became.

Morning:

What do you need to express before you Kick the Sh*t out of this day?

What Good Sh*t do you want to feel during the day?

Challenges you expect to face? How can you handle them?

Night:

What was the Good Sh*t of the day?

What was the Bad Sh*t of the day?

How will i make tomorrow better?

Morning:

What do you need to express before you Kick the Sh*t out of this day?

What Good Sh*t do you want to feel during the day?

Challenges you expect to face? How can you handle them?

Night:

What was the Good Sh*t of the day?

What was the Bad Sh*t of the day?

How will i make tomorrow better?

How Many F*cks Are You Not Gonna Give Today?

Morning:

What do you need to express before you Kick the Sh*t out of this day?

What Good Sh*t do you want to feel during the day?

Challenges you expect to face? How can you handle them?

Night:

What was the Good Sh*t of the day?

What was the Bad Sh*t of the day?

How will i make tomorrow better?

Morning:

What do you need to express before you Kick the Sh*t out of this day?

What Good Sh*t do you want to feel during the day?

Challenges you expect to face? How can you handle them?

Night:

What was the Good Sh*t of the day?

What was the Bad Sh*t of the day?

How will i make tomorrow better?

Never play the Princess when you can be the Queen!

Morning:

What do you need to express before you Kick the Sh*t out of this day?

What Good Sh*t do you want to feel during the day?

Challenges you expect to face? How can you handle them?

Night:

What was the Good Sh*t of the day?

What was the Bad Sh*t of the day?

How will i make tomorrow better?

Morning:

What do you need to express before you Kick the Sh*t out of this day?

What Good Sh*t do you want to feel during the day?

Challenges you expect to face? How can you handle them?

Night:

What was the Good Sh*t of the day?

What was the Bad Sh*t of the day?

How will i make tomorrow better?

You are more powerful then you will ever know! Are you ready to own that?

Morning:

What do you need to express before you Kick the Sh*t out of this day?

What Good Sh*t do you want to feel during the day?

Challenges you expect to face? How can you handle them?

Night:

What was the Good Sh*t of the day?

What was the Bad Sh*t of the day?

How will i make tomorrow better?

Morning:

What do you need to express before you Kick the Sh*t out of this day?

What Good Sh*t do you want to feel during the day?

Challenges you expect to face? How can you handle them?

Night:

What was the Good Sh*t of the day?

What was the Bad Sh*t of the day?

How will i make tomorrow better?

How will I be the Baddest B*tch I Can Be today?

Morning:

What do you need to express before you Kick the Sh*t out of this day?

What Good Sh*t do you want to feel during the day?

Challenges you expect to face? How can you handle them?

Night:

What was the Good Sh*t of the day?

What was the Bad Sh*t of the day?

How will i make tomorrow better?

Morning:

What do you need to express before you Kick the Sh*t out of this day?

What Good Sh*t do you want to feel during the day?

Challenges you expect to face? How can you handle them?

Night:

What was the Good Sh*t of the day?

What was the Bad Sh*t of the day?

How will i make tomorrow better?

Love!

Morning:

What do you need to express before you Kick the Sh*t out of this day?

_____

What Good Sh*t do you want to feel during the day?

_____

_____

Challenges you expect to face? How can you handle them?

_____

_____

Night:

What was the Good Sh*t of the day?

_____

_____

What was the Bad Sh*t of the day?

_____

_____

How will i make tomorrow better?

_____

_____

Morning:

What do you need to express before you Kick the Sh*t out of this day?

What Good Sh*t do you want to feel during the day?

Challenges you expect to face? How can you handle them?

Night:

What was the Good Sh*t of the day?

What was the Bad Sh*t of the day?

How will i make tomorrow better?

Remember How Far You've Come and Keep Looking into the Future...

Morning:

What do you need to express before you Kick the Sh*t out of this day?

What Good Sh*t do you want to feel during the day?

Challenges you expect to face? How can you handle them?

Night:

What was the Good Sh*t of the day?

What was the Bad Sh*t of the day?

How will i make tomorrow better?

Morning:

What do you need to express before you Kick the Sh*t out of this day?

What Good Sh*t do you want to feel during the day?

Challenges you expect to face? How can you handle them?

Night:

What was the Good Sh*t of the day?

What was the Bad Sh*t of the day?

How will i make tomorrow better?

Life is tough but damn, So are you Girl!

Morning:

What do you need to express before you Kick the Sh*t out of this day?

What Good Sh*t do you want to feel during the day?

Challenges you expect to face? How can you handle them?

Night:

What was the Good Sh*t of the day?

What was the Bad Sh*t of the day?

How will i make tomorrow better?

Morning:

What do you need to express before you kick the Sh*t out of this day?

What Good Sh*t do you want to feel during the day?

Challenges you expect to face? How can you handle them?

Night:

What was the Good Sh*t of the day?

What was the Bad Sh*t of the day?

How will i make tomorrow better?

Remember Your "Why?"

Morning:

What do you need to express before you Kick the Sh*t out of this day?

What Good Sh*t do you want to feel during the day?

Challenges you expect to face? How can you handle them?

Night:

What was the Good Sh*t of the day?

What was the Bad Sh*t of the day?

How will i make tomorrow better?

Morning:

What do you need to express before you Kick the Sh*t out of this day?

_____

_____

What Good Sh*t do you want to feel during the day?

_____

_____

Challenges you expect to face? How can you handle them?

_____

_____

Night:

What was the Good Sh*t of the day?

_____

_____

What was the Bad Sh*t of the day?

_____

_____

How will i make tomorrow better?

_____

_____

Believe you can B*tch
And You're Half Way There!

Morning:

What do you need to express before you Kick the Sh*t out of this day?

What Good Sh*t do you want to feel during the day?

Challenges you expect to face? How can you handle them?

Night:

What was the Good Sh*t of the day?

What was the Bad Sh*t of the day?

How will i make tomorrow better?

Morning:

What do you need to express before you Kick the Sh*t out of this day?

What Good Sh*t do you want to feel during the day?

Challenges you expect to face? How can you handle them?

Night:

What was the Good Sh*t of the day?

What was the Bad Sh*t of the day?

How will i make tomorrow better?

Owning Your Story is the Bravest Thing You'll Ever Do.

Morning:

What do you need to express before you Kick the Sh*t out of this day?

What Good Sh*t do you want to feel during the day?

Challenges you expect to face? How can you handle them?

Night:

What was the Good Sh*t of the day?

What was the Bad Sh*t of the day?

How will i make tomorrow better?

Morning:

What do you need to express before you Kick the Sh*t out of this day?

What Good Sh*t do you want to feel during the day?

Challenges you expect to face? How can you handle them?

Night:

What was the Good Sh*t of the day?

What was the Bad Sh*t of the day?

How will i make tomorrow better?

You a kick-the-door-down-and -take-names-kinda-Bad-Ass-B*tch!

Morning:

What do you need to express before you Kick the Sh*t out of this day?

What Good Sh*t do you want to feel during the day?

Challenges you expect to face? How can you handle them?

Night:

What was the Good Sh*t of the day?

What was the Bad Sh*t of the day?

How will i make tomorrow better?

Morning:

What do you need to express before you Kick the Sh*t out of this day?

What Good Sh*t do you want to feel during the day?

Challenges you expect to face? How can you handle them?

Night:

What was the Good Sh*t of the day?

What was the Bad Sh*t of the day?

How will i make tomorrow better?

Everyday is a Miracle. What Are You Going To Do With Yours Today?

Morning:

What do you need to express before you Kick the Sh*t out of this day?

What Good Sh*t do you want to feel during the day?

Challenges you expect to face? How can you handle them?

Night:

What was the Good Sh*t of the day?

What was the Bad Sh*t of the day?

How will i make tomorrow better?

Morning:

What do you need to express before you Kick the Sh*t out of this day?

What Good Sh*t do you want to feel during the day?

Challenges you expect to face? How can you handle them?

Night:

What was the Good Sh*t of the day?

What was the Bad Sh*t of the day?

How will i make tomorrow better?

Kind Heart, Fierce Mind, Brave Spirit!

Morning:

What do you need to express before you Kick the Sh*t out of this day?

What Good Sh*t do you want to feel during the day?

Challenges you expect to face? How can you handle them?

Night:

What was the Good Sh*t of the day?

What was the Bad Sh*t of the day?

How will i make tomorrow better?

Morning:

What do you need to express before you Kick the Sh*t out of this day?

What Good Sh*t do you want to feel during the day?

Challenges you expect to face? How can you handle them?

Night:

What was the Good Sh*t of the day?

What was the Bad Sh*t of the day?

How will i make tomorrow better?

How Can I Make Today the Best Day it Can Be For Me?

Morning:

What do you need to express before you Kick the Sh*t out of this day?

What Good Sh*t do you want to feel during the day?

Challenges you expect to face? How can you handle them?

Night:

What was the Good Sh*t of the day?

What was the Bad Sh*t of the day?

How will i make tomorrow better?

Morning:

What do you need to express before you Kick the Sh*t out of this day?

What Good Sh*t do you want to feel during the day?

Challenges you expect to face? How can you handle them?

Night:

What was the Good Sh*t of the day?

What was the Bad Sh*t of the day?

How will i make tomorrow better?

Don't Betray Yourself B*tch! Your Heart and Soul is Too Precious for Any So Called Gain From It.

Morning:

What do you need to express before you Kick the Sh*t out of this day?

What Good Sh*t do you want to feel during the day?

Challenges you expect to face? How can you handle them?

Night:

What was the Good Sh*t of the day?

What was the Bad Sh*t of the day?

How will i make tomorrow better?

Morning:

What do you need to express before you Kick the Sh*t out of this day?

What Good Sh*t do you want to feel during the day?

Challenges you expect to face? How can you handle them?

Night:

What was the Good Sh*t of the day?

What was the Bad Sh*t of the day?

How will i make tomorrow better?

Ambitious as F*ck!

Morning:

What do you need to express before you Kick the Sh*t out of this day?

What Good Sh*t do you want to feel during the day?

Challenges you expect to face? How can you handle them?

Night:

What was the Good Sh*t of the day?

What was the Bad Sh*t of the day?

How will i make tomorrow better?

Morning:

What do you need to express before you Kick the Sh*t out of this day?

What Good Sh*t do you want to feel during the day?

Challenges you expect to face? How can you handle them?

Night:

What was the Good Sh*t of the day?

What was the Bad Sh*t of the day?

How will i make tomorrow better?

Bad hair, Don't care, Let Them Stop and Stare, I've Got No F*cks to Give i Swear!

Morning:

What do you need to express before you Kick the Sh*t out of this day?

What Good Sh*t do you want to feel during the day?

Challenges you expect to face? How can you handle them?

Night:

What was the Good Sh*t of the day?

What was the Bad Sh*t of the day?

How will i make tomorrow better?

Morning:

What do you need to express before you Kick the Sh*t out of this day?

What Good Sh*t do you want to feel during the day?

Challenges you expect to face? How can you handle them?

Night:

What was the Good Sh*t of the day?

What was the Bad Sh*t of the day?

How will i make tomorrow better?

How Will i Be The Best Version Of Me Today?

Morning:

What do you need to express before you Kick the Sh*t out of this day?

What Good Sh*t do you want to feel during the day?

Challenges you expect to face? How can you handle them?

Night:

What was the Good Sh*t of the day?

What was the Bad Sh*t of the day?

How will i make tomorrow better?

Morning:

What do you need to express before you Kick the Sh*t out of this day?

What Good Sh*t do you want to feel during the day?

Challenges you expect to face? How can you handle them?

Night:

What was the Good Sh*t of the day?

What was the Bad Sh*t of the day?

How will i make tomorrow better?

Nothing Worth Having Ever Comes Easy.
Bad B*tches Embrace This!

Morning:

What do you need to express before you Kick the Sh*t out of this day?

What Good Sh*t do you want to feel during the day?

Challenges you expect to face? How can you handle them?

Night:

What was the Good Sh*t of the day?

What was the Bad Sh*t of the day?

How will i make tomorrow better?

Morning:

What do you need to express before you Kick the Sh*t out of this day?

What Good Sh*t do you want to feel during the day?

Challenges you expect to face? How can you handle them?

Night:

What was the Good Sh*t of the day?

What was the Bad Sh*t of the day?

How will i make tomorrow better?

What Beautiful Sh*t Could Happen Today?

Morning:

What do you need to express before you Kick the Sh*t out of this day?

What Good Sh*t do you want to feel during the day?

Challenges you expect to face? How can you handle them?

Night:

What was the Good Sh*t of the day?

What was the Bad Sh*t of the day?

How will i make tomorrow better?

Morning:

What do you need to express before you Kick the Sh*t out of this day?

_____

What Good Sh*t do you want to feel during the day?

_____

Challenges you expect to face? How can you handle them?

_____

Night:

What was the Good Sh*t of the day?

_____

What was the Bad Sh*t of the day?

_____

How will i make tomorrow better?

_____

Don't Wish For it, Work for it!

Morning:

What do you need to express before you Kick the Sh*t out of this day?

What Good Sh*t do you want to feel during the day?

Challenges you expect to face? How can you handle them?

Night:

What was the Good Sh*t of the day?

What was the Bad Sh*t of the day?

How will i make tomorrow better?

Morning:

What do you need to express before you Kick the Sh*t out of this day?

What Good Sh*t do you want to feel during the day?

Challenges you expect to face? How can you handle them?

Night:

What was the Good Sh*t of the day?

What was the Bad Sh*t of the day?

How will i make tomorrow better?

She Remembered Who She Was And The Game Changed.

Morning:

What do you need to express before you Kick the Sh*t out of this day?

What Good Sh*t do you want to feel during the day?

Challenges you expect to face? How can you handle them?

Night:

What was the Good Sh*t of the day?

What was the Bad Sh*t of the day?

How will i make tomorrow better?

Morning:

What do you need to express before you Kick the Sh*t out of this day?

What Good Sh*t do you want to feel during the day?

Challenges you expect to face? How can you handle them?

Night:

What was the Good Sh*t of the day?

What was the Bad Sh*t of the day?

How will i make tomorrow better?

Go Get It Today!

Morning:

What do you need to express before you Kick the Sh*t out of this day?

What Good Sh*t do you want to feel during the day?

Challenges you expect to face? How can you handle them?

Night:

What was the Good Sh*t of the day?

What was the Bad Sh*t of the day?

How will i make tomorrow better?

Morning:

What do you need to express before you Kick the Sh*t out of this day?

What Good Sh*t do you want to feel during the day?

Challenges you expect to face? How can you handle them?

Night:

What was the Good Sh*t of the day?

What was the Bad Sh*t of the day?

How will i make tomorrow better?

Forget Yesterday! You Start Anew Everyday. How Do You Want to Experience The World Today?

Morning:

What do you need to express before you Kick the Sh*t out of this day?

What Good Sh*t do you want to feel during the day?

Challenges you expect to face? How can you handle them?

Night:

What was the Good Sh*t of the day?

What was the Bad Sh*t of the day?

How will i make tomorrow better?

Morning:

What do you need to express before you Kick the Sh*t out of this day?

What Good Sh*t do you want to feel during the day?

Challenges you expect to face? How can you handle them?

Night:

What was the Good Sh*t of the day?

What was the Bad Sh*t of the day?

How will i make tomorrow better?

She is Clothed in Strength and Dignity.
Be that kinda Bad Ass B*tch Today.

Morning:

What do you need to express before you Kick the Sh*t out of this day?

What Good Sh*t do you want to feel during the day?

Challenges you expect to face? How can you handle them?

Night:

What was the Good Sh*t of the day?

What was the Bad Sh*t of the day?

How will i make tomorrow better?

Morning:

What do you need to express before you Kick the Sh*t out of this day?

What Good Sh*t do you want to feel during the day?

Challenges you expect to face? How can you handle them?

Night:

What was the Good Sh*t of the day?

What was the Bad Sh*t of the day?

How will i make tomorrow better?

You Can Change Things For Yourself. Just Believe!

Morning:

What do you need to express before you Kick the Sh*t out of this day?

What Good Sh*t do you want to feel during the day?

Challenges you expect to face? How can you handle them?

Night:

What was the Good Sh*t of the day?

What was the Bad Sh*t of the day?

How will i make tomorrow better?

Morning:

What do you need to express before you Kick the Sh*t out of this day?

What Good Sh*t do you want to feel during the day?

Challenges you expect to face? How can you handle them?

Night:

What was the Good Sh*t of the day?

What was the Bad Sh*t of the day?

How will i make tomorrow better?

What really matters to me deep in my Soul?

Morning:

What do you need to express before you Kick the Sh*t out of this day?

What Good Sh*t do you want to feel during the day?

Challenges you expect to face? How can you handle them?

Night:

What was the Good Sh*t of the day?

What was the Bad Sh*t of the day?

How will i make tomorrow better?

Morning:

What do you need to express before you Kick the Sh*t out of this day?

What Good Sh*t do you want to feel during the day?

Challenges you expect to face? How can you handle them?

Night:

What was the Good Sh*t of the day?

What was the Bad Sh*t of the day?

How will i make tomorrow better?

Design a Life You Love and Live It!
You So Deserve It.

Morning:

What do you need to express before you Kick the Sh*t out of this day?

What Good Sh*t do you want to feel during the day?

Challenges you expect to face? How can you handle them?

Night:

What was the Good Sh*t of the day?

What was the Bad Sh*t of the day?

How will i make tomorrow better?

Morning:

What do you need to express before you Kick the Sh*t out of this day?

What Good Sh*t do you want to feel during the day?

Challenges you expect to face? How can you handle them?

Night:

What was the Good Sh*t of the day?

What was the Bad Sh*t of the day?

How will i make tomorrow better?

Sometimes All You Need to do is Just Breathe!

Morning:

What do you need to express before you Kick the Sh*t out of this day?

What Good Sh*t do you want to feel during the day?

Challenges you expect to face? How can you handle them?

Night:

What was the Good Sh*t of the day?

What was the Bad Sh*t of the day?

How will i make tomorrow better?

Morning:

What do you need to express before you Kick the Sh*t out of this day?

What Good Sh*t do you want to feel during the day?

Challenges you expect to face? How can you handle them?

Night:

What was the Good Sh*t of the day?

What was the Bad Sh*t of the day?

How will i make tomorrow better?

How Can i Make The Little Girl Inside Of Me Happy Today?

Morning:

What do you need to express before you Kick the Sh*t out of this day?

What Good Sh*t do you want to feel during the day?

Challenges you expect to face? How can you handle them?

Night:

What was the Good Sh*t of the day?

What was the Bad Sh*t of the day?

How will i make tomorrow better?

Morning:

What do you need to express before you Kick the Sh*t out of this day?

What Good Sh*t do you want to feel during the day?

Challenges you expect to face? How can you handle them?

Night:

What was the Good Sh*t of the day?

What was the Bad Sh*t of the day?

How will i make tomorrow better?

Be The Girl Who Decided To Go For It!

Morning:

What do you need to express before you Kick the Sh*t out of this day?

What Good Sh*t do you want to feel during the day?

Challenges you expect to face? How can you handle them?

Night:

What was the Good Sh*t of the day?

What was the Bad Sh*t of the day?

How will i make tomorrow better?

Morning:

What do you need to express before you Kick the Sh*t out of this day?

What Good Sh*t do you want to feel during the day?

Challenges you expect to face? How can you handle them?

Night:

What was the Good Sh*t of the day?

What was the Bad Sh*t of the day?

How will i make tomorrow better?

A True Warrior : She's Got Brains and Beauty And Is Kind With Both!

Morning:

What do you need to express before you Kick the Sh*t out of this day?

What Good Sh*t do you want to feel during the day?

Challenges you expect to face? How can you handle them?

Night:

What was the Good Sh*t of the day?

What was the Bad Sh*t of the day?

How will i make tomorrow better?

Morning:

What do you need to express before you Kick the Sh*t out of this day?

What Good Sh*t do you want to feel during the day?

Challenges you expect to face? How can you handle them?

Night:

What was the Good Sh*t of the day?

What was the Bad Sh*t of the day?

How will i make tomorrow better?

If I Had to Live Today on Repeat, What One Thing Would I Want to Make Sure I Experience?

Morning:

What do you need to express before you Kick the Sh*t out of this day?

What Good Sh*t do you want to feel during the day?

Challenges you expect to face? How can you handle them?

Night:

What was the Good Sh*t of the day?

What was the Bad Sh*t of the day?

How will i make tomorrow better?

Notes

Notes

Notes

If you enjoyed the journal, please take a moment to leave a review on the website and let me know if you'd like a second edition with some more tough love inspiration! :)

And please keep an eye out for some of our other fun planners and journals listed under our author name :

"GoGirl Press"

1. F*ck Me, I'm Gonna Do This Diet and Exercise Sh*t : A Food Diary and Fitness Planner For Some Real F*cking Weight Loss!

2. Grateful As F*ck!:A 3 Minute Gratitude Journal For One Blessed B*tch!

Keep Slaying Each Day!

Made in the USA
Columbia, SC
16 July 2019